# ACCENT ON ACHIEVEMENT

John
M
**Williams**

## The "Keys" to Success: Progressive Technical & Rhythmic Studies in all 12 Major and 12 Minor Keys

Dear Band Student:

Congratulations on completing the first two books of **ACCENT ON ACHIEVEMENT**. Book 3 will help you to develop the musical and technical skills necessary for a lifetime of great music-making. Your "Keys" to success include scales, exercises and fun tunes in all 12 major and 12 minor keys. You'll learn new rhythms and meters, and also improve your tone and intonation while playing a rich variety of chorales. With diligent practice, there's no end to what you can accomplish! We wish you the best in your quest for musical excellence.

John O'Reilly

Mark Williams

Instrument photos (cover and page 1) are courtesy of Yamaha Corporation of America.

## ACCENT ON CONCERT B♭ MAJOR

### CHORALE: CHILDREN'S PRAYER from "HANSEL AND GRETEL"

Engelbert Humperdinck
(1854–1921)

### B♭ MAJOR SCALE (CONCERT B♭)

### INTERVAL WORKOUT

### SCALE STUDY

### CHROMATIC SCALE

## ACCENT ON RHYTHM: $\frac{9}{8}$ Time

## MORNING HAS BROKEN

Irish Folk Song

## ACCENT ON RHYTHM: $\frac{12}{8}$ Time

## ANDANTE CANTABILE from "SYMPHONY NO. 5"

Peter I. Tchaikovsky
(1840–1893)

# ACCENT ON CONCERT G MINOR

### CHORALE: BASED ON A THEME BY NEUMARK

Johann Sebastian Bach
(1685–1750)

### G MELODIC MINOR SCALE (CONCERT G)

### INTERVAL WORKOUT

*See Position Chart on page 38.

### SCALE STUDY

### G HARMONIC MINOR SCALE (CONCERT G)

# ACCENT ON RHYTHM: 3/2 Time

**15**
Count: 1 & 2 & 3 (e) & a

## RONDO

Henry Purcell
(1659–1695)

**16** Maestoso

*Fine*

*D. C. al Fine*

## THE WILD HORSEMAN

Robert Schumann
(1810–1856)

**17** Allegro

*Fine*

*D. C. al Fine*

## ACCENT ON CONCERT E♭ MAJOR

### CHORALE: BE THOU MY VISION

Moderato

Traditional Irish Melody

### E♭ MAJOR SCALE (CONCERT E♭)

### INTERVAL WORKOUT

### SCALE STUDY

### CHROMATIC SCALE

## **A**CCENT ON RHYTHM: ♪♩.

**23** Count: 1 & 2 & 1 e(&a)2 &

## THE KEEL ROW

English/Scottish Folk Song

**Allegretto**

**24** *mf*

*f*

## **A**CCENT ON RHYTHM: ♫♪♩ and ♫♫♪♫

**25** Count: 1 e(&)a 2 & 1 & a (2) e &

## PETITE OISEAU

Traditional

**Moderato**

**26** *mp*

*mf*

# ACCENT ON CONCERT C MINOR

### CHORALE: PRELUDE IN C MINOR

Frèdèric Chopin
(1810–1849)

### C MELODIC MINOR SCALE (CONCERT C)

### INTERVAL WORKOUT

### SCALE STUDY

### C HARMONIC MINOR SCALE (CONCERT C)

## ACCENT ON RHYTHM:

**32** Count: 1 trip-let 2 3 4 trip-let

## THREE WAYS TO SWING IT

Allegro

**33** *mf*

Swing feel ( ♪♪ = ♩ ♪ )

## ACCENT ON RHYTHM: *Swing Eighth Notes*

Swing feel ( ♪♪ = ♩ ♪ )

**34**

## THE BATTLE OF JERICHO

Allegro – Swing feel ( ♪♪ = ♩ ♪ )

American Spiritual

**35** *f*

Fine

D. C. al Fine

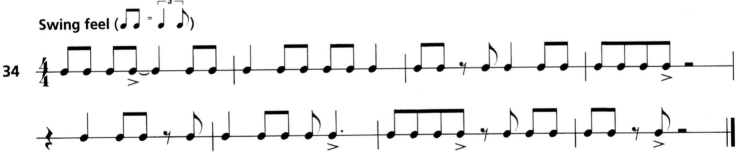

## ACCENT ON CONCERT F MAJOR

### CHORALE: SINE NOMINE
**Maestoso**

Ralph Vaughan Williams
(1872–1958)

36

*mf*

*f*

*rit.*

*mf*

### F MAJOR SCALE (CONCERT F)

37

*See Position Chart on page 38.

### INTERVAL WORKOUT

38

*See Position Chart on page 38.

### SCALE STUDY

39

### CHROMATIC SCALE

40

# Accent on Rhythm: ♪♪ in 6/8 Time

41

Count: 1   2   &   3   4   &   5   6

## The Irish Washerwoman

Traditional

Allegro

42

*mf*

1.

2.

1.

2.

## Lip Slur/Flexibility Study

43

*mp*

# ACCENT ON CONCERT D MINOR

## CHORALE: PICARDY

Andante

17th Century French Melody

## D MELODIC MINOR SCALE (CONCERT D)

## INTERVAL WORKOUT

## SCALE STUDY

## D HARMONIC MINOR SCALE (CONCERT D)

## ACCENT ON RHYTHM: (dotted eighth, sixteenth, eighth) in 6/8 Time

49
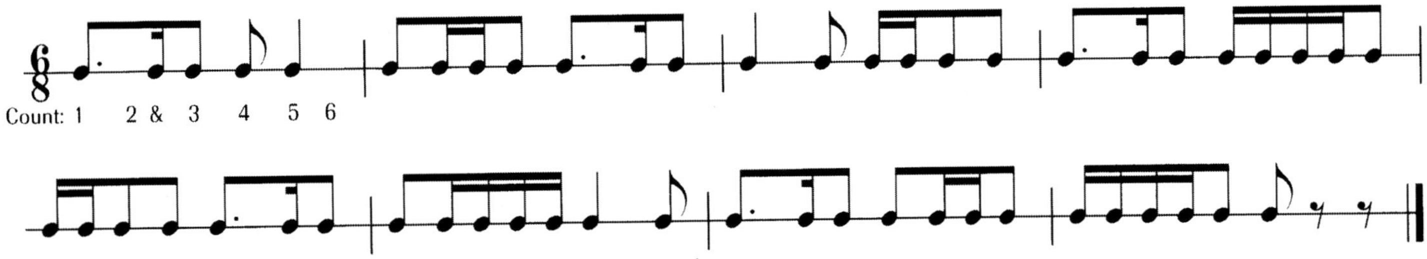
Count: 1 2 & 3 4 5 6

### GREENSLEEVES

English Folk Song

**Andante**

50
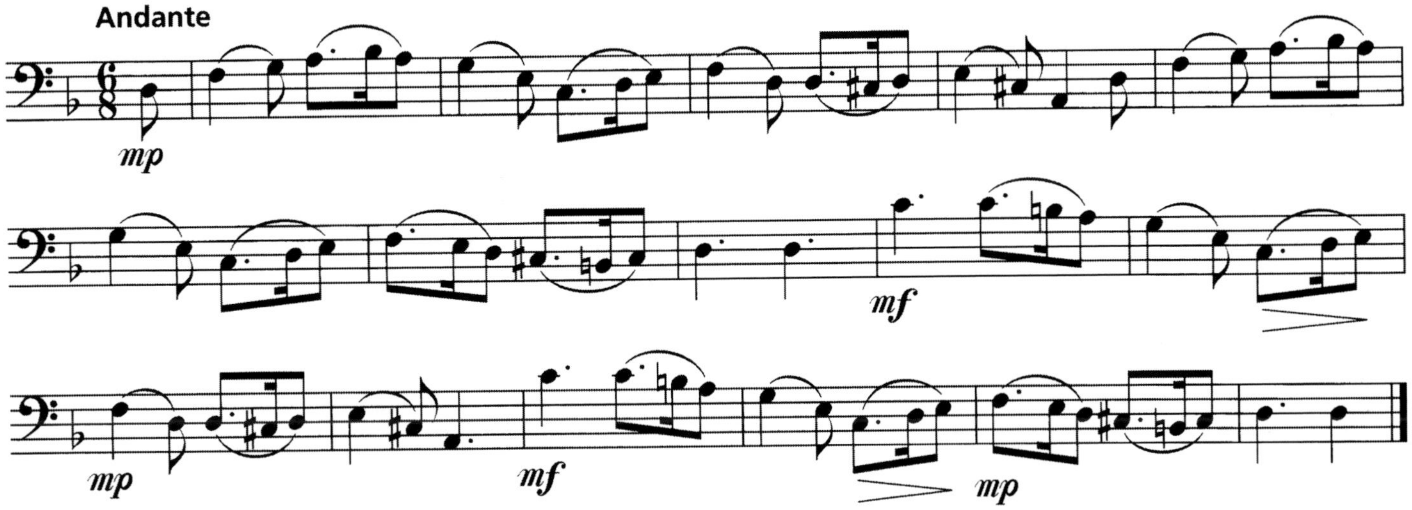
mp
mf
mp
mf
mp

## ACCENT ON RHYTHM: (Sixteenth Rest)

51
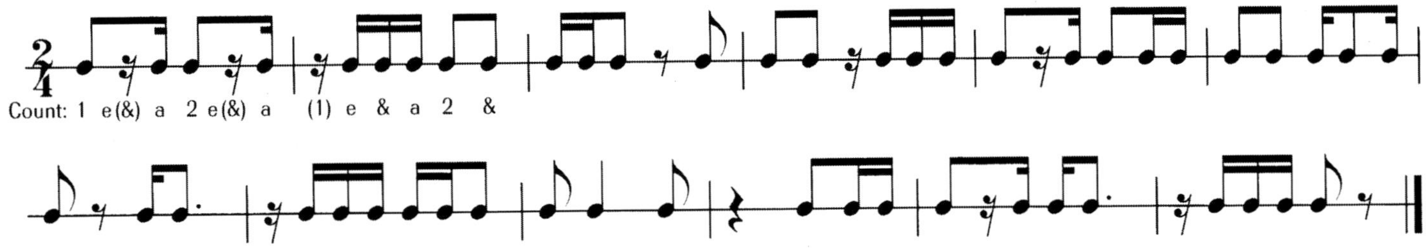
Count: 1 e(&) a 2 e(&) a (1) e & a 2 &

### LA CUMPARSITA

G. Matos Rodriguez
(1897–1948)

**Moderato**

52
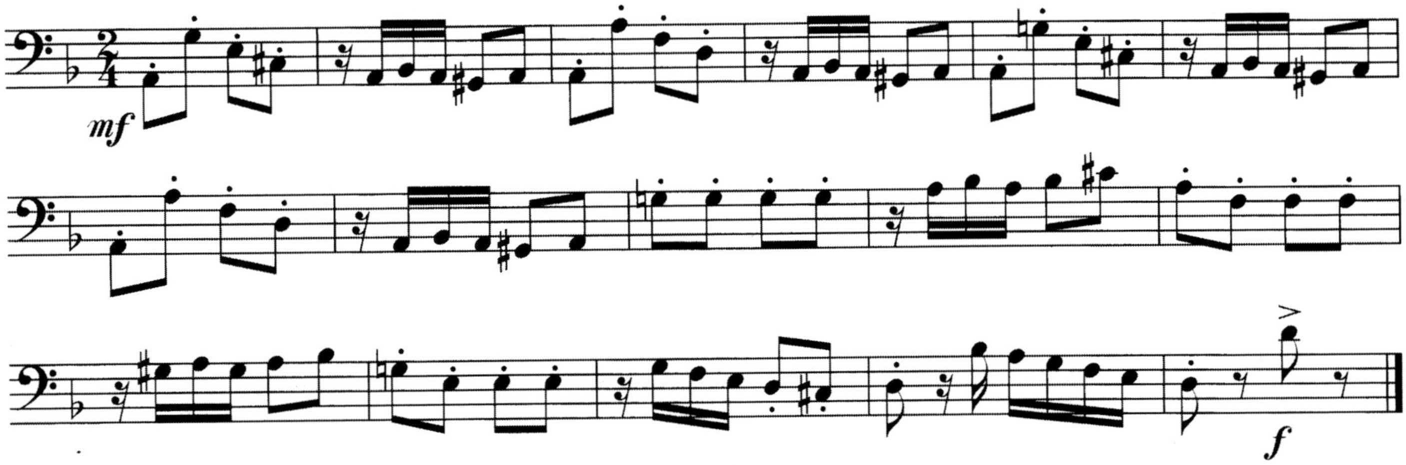
mf
f

# ACCENT ON CONCERT A♭ MAJOR

### CHORALE: HOW FIRM A FOUNDATION

Moderato

Early American Melody

### A♭ MAJOR SCALE (CONCERT A♭)

*See Position Chart on page 38.

### INTERVAL WORKOUT

### SCALE STUDY

### CHROMATIC SCALE

*See Position Chart on page 38.

# ACCENT ON RHYTHM: $\frac{5}{4}$ and $\frac{6}{4}$ Time

**PROMENADE from "PICTURES AT AN EXHIBITION"**

Modest Mussorgsky
(1839–1881)

Moderato

**WALTZ from "SYMPHONY No. 6"**

Peter I. Tchaikovsky
(1840–1893)

Allegretto

# ACCENT ON CONCERT F MINOR

## CHORALE: THE GOD OF ABRAHAM PRAISE

Moderato

Hebrew Folk Song

**61**

## F MELODIC MINOR SCALE (CONCERT F)

**62**

## INTERVAL WORKOUT

**63**

*See Position Chart on page 38.

## SCALE STUDY

**64**

## F HARMONIC MINOR SCALE (CONCERT F)

**65**

**A**CCENT ON RHYTHM:

66

Think: 1 2 3 4 5 6    1 2 3 4 5 6

## SOMETIMES I FEEL LIKE A MOTHERLESS CHILD

American Spiritual

67  Largo

## TRIPLET TUNE

68  Maestoso

# ACCENT ON CONCERT C MAJOR

### CHORALE: IT IS WELL

Phillip Bliss
(1838–1876)

### C MAJOR SCALE (CONCERT C)

### INTERVAL WORKOUT

### SCALE STUDY

### CHROMATIC SCALE

# ACCENT ON RHYTHM: Changing Meters — $\frac{2}{4}$ through $\frac{6}{4}$

## SOLILOQUY
Andante

## LIP SLUR/FLEXIBILITY STUDY

## ACCENT ON CONCERT A MINOR

### CHORALE: BASED ON A THEME BY HASSLER

Johann Sebastian Bach
(1685–1750)

### A MELODIC MINOR SCALE (CONCERT A)

### INTERVAL WORKOUT

### SCALE STUDY

### A HARMONIC MINOR SCALE (CONCERT A)

**ACCENT ON RHYTHM:** ♩.. ♪

**82** 

Count: 1 & 2 (e&)a   3   &   4   &

## PRELUDE from "L'ARLESIENNE"

Georges Bizet
(1838–1875)

**Allegro**

**83** 

*f*

## CAPRICE NO. 24

Nicolo Paganini
(1782–1840)

**Allegretto**

**84** 

*f-p*

*mf-f*

## ACCENT ON CONCERT D♭ MAJOR

### CHORALE: LONDONDERRY AIR

Andante

Irish Folk Song

### D♭ MAJOR SCALE (CONCERT D♭)

### INTERVAL WORKOUT

### SCALE STUDY

### CHROMATIC SCALE

**A**CCENT ON RHYTHM: *Changing Meters* — §8 and ²4

## WASSAIL SONG

Traditional Carol

**Allegretto**

*mf*

**A**CCENT ON RHYTHM: *Changing Meters* — §8 and ¾

## FIESTA MARIACHI

**Allegro**

*mf*

*Fine*

*D. C. al Fine*

## ACCENT ON CONCERT B♭ MINOR

### CHORALE: KOMM, SÜSSER TOD

Johann Sebastian Bach
(1685–1750)

# ACCENT ON RHYTHM: ⅝ Time

99

Count: 1 2 3 4 5

## FUN WITH FIVE

100

Moderato

mp

mf

mp

mf

# ACCENT ON RHYTHM: Changing Meters with ⅜ , ⅝

101
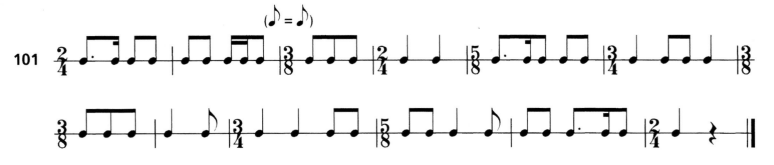

(♪ = ♪)

## VARIATIONS ON A STAR SONG

102

Moderato (♪ = ♪)

mf

Count: 1 2 3 4 5 6 7

## ACCENT ON CONCERT G MAJOR

### G MAJOR SCALE (CONCERT G)

### INTERVAL WORKOUT

### CHROMATIC SCALE

### LA CUCARACHA

Mexican Folk Song

**Allegretto**

### AULD LANG SYNE

Scottish Folk Song

**Andante**

# ACCENT ON CONCERT E MINOR

## E MELODIC MINOR SCALE (CONCERT E)

108

## INTERVAL WORKOUT

109

## E HARMONIC MINOR SCALE (CONCERT E)

110

## LA CINQUANTAINE

J. Gabriel-Marie
(1852–1928)

**Allegretto**

111

## ACCENT ON CONCERT G♭ MAJOR

### G♭ MAJOR SCALE (CONCERT G♭)

**112**

### INTERVAL WORKOUT

**113**

### CHROMATIC SCALE

**114**

### MICHAEL, ROW THE BOAT ASHORE

Andante

American Spiritual

**115**

*mp*

### MARCH OF THE MEN OF HARLECH

Welsh Folk Song

Moderato

**116**

*f*

# ACCENT ON CONCERT E♭ MINOR

### E♭ MELODIC MINOR SCALE (CONCERT E♭)

**117**

### INTERVAL WORKOUT

**118**

### E♭ HARMONIC MINOR SCALE (CONCERT E♭)

**119**

### THEME from "SWAN LAKE"

Peter I. Tchaikovsky
(1840–1893)

**Andante**

**120**

# ACCENT ON CONCERT D MAJOR

### D MAJOR SCALE (CONCERT D)

121

### INTERVAL WORKOUT

122

### CHROMATIC SCALE

123

### ALLELUIA

17th Century Melody

Moderato

124

### SHENANDOAH

American Folk Song

Adagio

125

# ACCENT ON CONCERT B MINOR

### B MELODIC MINOR SCALE (CONCERT B)

**126**

### INTERVAL WORKOUT

**127**

### B HARMONIC MINOR SCALE (CONCERT B)

**128**

### HATIKVAH

Israeli National Anthem

**Maestoso**

**129**

## ACCENT ON CONCERT A MAJOR

### A MAJOR SCALE (CONCERT A)

**130**

### INTERVAL WORKOUT

**131**

### CHROMATIC SCALE

**132**

### BINGO

American Folk Song

**133**

Allegro

$f$

### MY BONNIE LIES OVER THE OCEAN

Traditional

**134**

Moderato

$mf$

## ACCENT ON CONCERT F♯/G♭ MINOR

### F♯ MELODIC MINOR SCALE (CONCERT F♯)

**135**

### INTERVAL WORKOUT

**136**

### F♯ HARMONIC MINOR SCALE (CONCERT F♯)

**137**

### THEME from "SCHEHERAZADE"

Nicolai Rimsky-Korsakov
(1844–1908)

**Moderato**

**138**

*mf*

*f*

## ACCENT ON CONCERT C♭ MAJOR

### C♭ MAJOR SCALE (CONCERT C♭)

**139**

### INTERVAL WORKOUT

**140**

### CHROMATIC SCALE

**141**

### THE BLUEBELLS OF SCOTLAND

Scottish Folk Song

**142**

### BEAUTIFUL DREAMER

Stephen Foster
(1826–1864)

**143**

# Accent on Concert A♭ Minor

## A♭ Melodic Minor Scale (Concert A♭)

**144**

## Interval Workout

**145**

## A♭ Harmonic Minor Scale (Concert A♭)

**146**

## Hava Nagila

Hebrew Folk Song

**147**

# ACCENT ON CONCERT E MAJOR

### E MAJOR SCALE (CONCERT E)

148

### INTERVAL WORKOUT

149

### CHROMATIC SCALE

150

### HOME ON THE RANGE

American Folk Song

Moderato

151

mf

# ACCENT ON CONCERT C#/Db MINOR

### C# MELODIC MINOR SCALE (CONCERT C#)

**152**

### INTERVAL WORKOUT

**153**

### C# HARMONIC MINOR SCALE (CONCERT C#)

**154**

### WE THREE KINGS

Traditional Carol

**Moderato**

**155**

# TROMBONE POSITION CHART

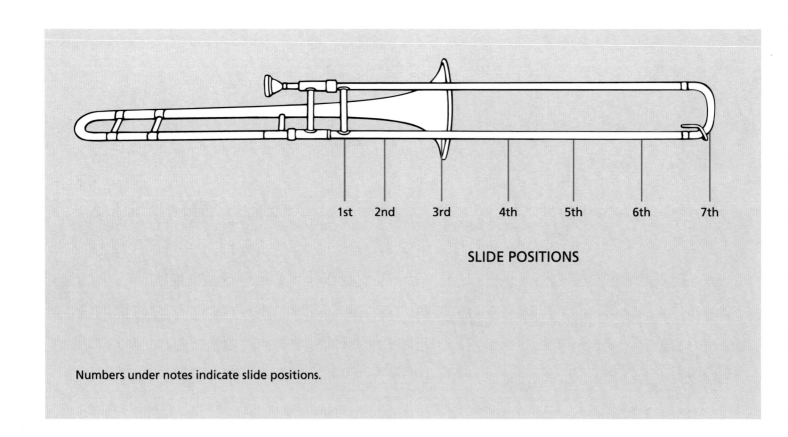

1st   2nd   3rd   4th   5th   6th   7th

## SLIDE POSITIONS

Numbers under notes indicate slide positions.

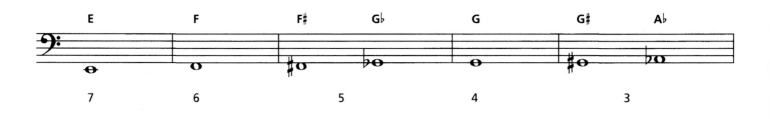

E — 7   F — 6   F# / G♭ — 5   G — 4   G# / A♭ — 3

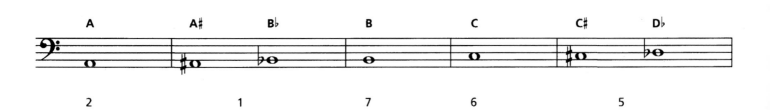

A — 2   A# / B♭ — 1   B — 7   C — 6   C# / D♭ — 5

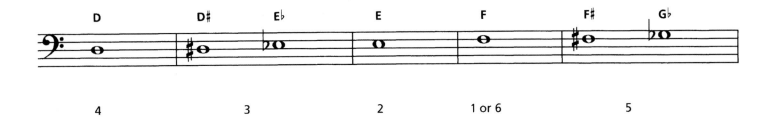

| D | D# | E♭ | E | F | F# | G♭ |
|---|----|----|---|---|----|----|
| 4 | 3 | | 2 | 1 or 6 | 5 | |

| G | G# | A♭ | A | A# | B♭ | B |
|---|----|----|---|----|----|---|
| 4 | 3 | | 2 | 1 or 5 | 4 | |

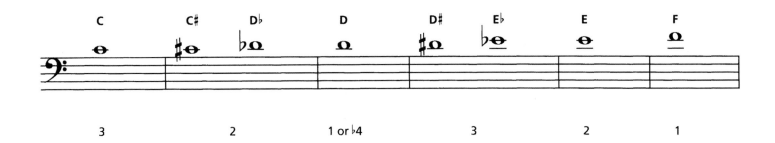

| C | C# | D♭ | D | D# | E♭ | E | F |
|---|----|----|---|----|----|---|---|
| 3 | 2 | 1 or ♭4 | 3 | | 2 | 1 | |

| F# | G♭ | G | G# | A♭ | A | B♭ |
|----|----|---|----|----|---|----|
| #3 | #2 | 3 | | 2 | 1 | |

# HOME PRACTICE RECORD

| Week | Date | ASSIGNMENT | Mon | Tue | Wed | Thur | Fri | Sat | Sun | Total | Parent Signature |
|---|---|---|---|---|---|---|---|---|---|---|---|
| 1 | | | | | | | | | | | |
| 2 | | | | | | | | | | | |
| 3 | | | | | | | | | | | |
| 4 | | | | | | | | | | | |
| 5 | | | | | | | | | | | |
| 6 | | | | | | | | | | | |
| 7 | | | | | | | | | | | |
| 8 | | | | | | | | | | | |
| 9 | | | | | | | | | | | |
| 10 | | | | | | | | | | | |
| 11 | | | | | | | | | | | |
| 12 | | | | | | | | | | | |
| 13 | | | | | | | | | | | |
| 14 | | | | | | | | | | | |
| 15 | | | | | | | | | | | |
| 16 | | | | | | | | | | | |
| 17 | | | | | | | | | | | |
| 18 | | | | | | | | | | | |
| 19 | | | | | | | | | | | |
| 20 | | | | | | | | | | | |
| 21 | | | | | | | | | | | |
| 22 | | | | | | | | | | | |
| 23 | | | | | | | | | | | |
| 24 | | | | | | | | | | | |
| 25 | | | | | | | | | | | |
| 26 | | | | | | | | | | | |
| 27 | | | | | | | | | | | |
| 28 | | | | | | | | | | | |
| 29 | | | | | | | | | | | |
| 30 | | | | | | | | | | | |
| 31 | | | | | | | | | | | |
| 32 | | | | | | | | | | | |
| 33 | | | | | | | | | | | |
| 34 | | | | | | | | | | | |
| 35 | | | | | | | | | | | |
| 36 | | | | | | | | | | | |